Holidays

Thanksgiving

by Rebecca Pettiford

Bullfrog Books

Ideas for Parents and Teachers

Bullfrog Books let children practice reading informational text at the earliest reading levels. Repetition, familiar words, and photo labels support early readers.

Before Reading

- Discuss the cover photo. What does it tell them?

- Look at the picture glossary together. Read and discuss the words.

Read the Book

- "Walk" through the book and look at the photos. Let the child ask questions. Point out the photo labels.

- Read the book to the child, or have him or her read independently.

After Reading

- Prompt the child to think more. Ask: Does your family celebrate Thanksgiving? What sorts of things do you see when it's Thanksgiving?

Bullfrog Books are published by Jump!
5357 Penn Avenue South
Minneapolis, MN 55419
www.jumplibrary.com

Library of Congress Cataloging-in-Publication Data

Pettiford, Rebecca.
  Thanksgiving / by Rebecca Pettiford.
    pages cm. — (Holidays)
  ISBN 978-1-62031-186-8 (hardcover: alk. paper) —
  ISBN 978-1-62496-273-8 (ebook)
  1. Thanksgiving Day—Juvenile literature. I. Title.
  GT4975.P48 2016
  394.2649—dc23

                                                    2014041412

Editor: Jenny Fretland VanVoorst
Series Designer: Ellen Huber
Book Designer: Michelle Sonnek
Photo Researcher: Michelle Sonnek

Photo Credits: All photos by Shutterstock except: age fotostock, 15; Alamy, 8–9, 13, 23tr, 23bl, 23br; Corbis, 20–21; iStock, 4, 5, 10–11, 13, 14–15, 22bl, 23tl; Thinkstock, 12, 19, 22br, 24.

Printed in the United States of America at Corporate Graphics in North Mankato, Minnesota.

Table of Contents

What Is Thanksgiving?

Thanksgiving is
an American holiday.

It is in November.

It is on the fourth Thursday.

What do we do?

Our family gets together.

We remember the first Thanksgiving.

early
settlers

native
people

8

It was long ago.

Who was there?

Early settlers and native people.

They ate a big feast.

We make a lot of food.
Yum! What smells good?
Turkey!

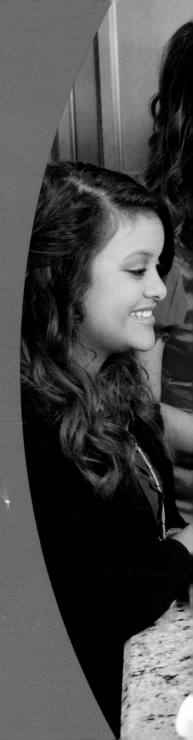

We see a parade. It is on TV.

12

Look! A float!

Rae sets the table.
Wow! It looks like fall.

15

It is time to eat.

We sit at the table.

We give thanks
for our family.

Dad cuts the turkey.

Troy likes corn.

Jess likes pumpkin pie.

19

We are full.

We take a nap.

Happy Thanksgiving!

Symbols of Thanksgiving

family

turkey

Thanksgiving table

pumpkin pie

Picture Glossary

feast
A big meal that people eat to honor a special day or event.

native people
People who were born in the country in which they live.

float
An object that is attached to a truck's platform and shown in a parade.

settlers
People who move from one place to another and live there.

23

Index

To Learn More

Learning more is as easy as 1, 2, 3.

1) Go to www.factsurfer.com

2) Enter "Thanksgiving" into the search box.

3) Click the "Surf" button to see a list of websites.

With factsurfer.com, finding more information is just a click away.